SCHOLASTIC

Standardized Test Practice
WRITING

Grades 3–4

25 Reproducible Mini-Tests That Help Students
Prepare for and Succeed on Standardized Tests

Michael Priestley

NEW YORK • TORONTO • LONDON • AUCKLAND • SYDNEY
MEXICO CITY • NEW DELHI • HONG KONG • BUENOS AIRES

Editor: Maria L. Chang
Cover design by Brian LaRossa
Cover photograph © Corbis. All Rights Reserved.
Interior design by Kathy Massaro
Interior illustrations by Michelle Dorenkamp
Photo, page 12: © Scott Bales/Icon SMI/Corbis
Photo, page 22: © Time Life Pictures/Gettyimages

ISBN-13: 978-0-545-06401–9
ISBN-10: 0-545-06401–5
Copyright © 2008 by Michael Priestley
All rights reserved.
Printed in the U.S.A.

1 2 3 4 5 6 7 8 9 10   40   15 14 13 12 11 10 09 08

Contents

Introduction

*E*very year, students in many states participate in writing assessments that include both a writing prompt and a writing test. The writing tests often comprise a series of written passages and multiple-choice questions testing composition, grammar, usage, and mechanics. The purpose of this book is to help you prepare students for these kinds of writing tests by improving their skills in prewriting, drafting, revising, and editing.

What You Will Find in This Book

The writing practice activities in this book reflect the different kinds of tests used in many parts of the United States. The exercises and writing skills included in this book are based on an analysis and correlation of statewide assessments and content standards in ten states. Formats and types of items vary from one practice to another to reflect the formats used in different states. Writing skills covered in these activities include the following:

* **Prewriting** Planning, generating ideas, determining writer's purpose, organizing ideas, identifying sources of information, and using graphic organizers

* **Drafting & Revising** Developing main ideas and supporting details, organizing and sequencing information, providing text structure and coherence, using transition words and phrases, using precise words, and evaluating author's style

* **Editing & Proofreading** Using correct grammar, using complete sentences, combining sentences, capitalizing words correctly, using correct punctuation and spelling

This book provides 28 grade-appropriate writing practice activities, ranging from one page to four pages in length. Most of the activities include written passages presented as student-produced drafts. In Prewriting and Drafting & Revising, each activity has a set of three, four, or eight multiple-choice questions, depending on the length of the activity. The two Editing Practices, A and B, are four pages long and have 16 questions each.

How to Use This Book

I recommend using one or two practice activities with your students each week, or you may want to assign practice activities to fit with the particular writing skills you are teaching at a given time in the classroom. When students complete the activities, use the answer key (beginning on page 62) to score their responses. You may want to have students correct their own tests so they can see which questions they answered correctly and which ones they missed.

These practice activities will help you and your students determine how well they have learned particular skills and what additional instruction you might need to provide. On page 64, you will find a Student Score Record. You may want to make a copy of this page for each student, to keep track of their scores on all the practice activities and to see the progress they have made.

Name .... Date ....

Deanna plans to write a school paper. She starts by making these notes. Use the notes to answer questions 1–3.

Deanna's Notes

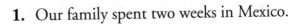

1. Our family spent two weeks in Mexico.
2. We went to Mexico City.
3. The city is very crowded and busy.
4. My brother loves to ride in taxis.
5. We went to the Yucatán.
6. We saw Mayan pyramids and villages.

1. **Which note is off topic and should be removed?**

Ⓐ Our family spent two weeks in Mexico.

Ⓑ We went to Mexico City.

Ⓒ My brother loves to ride in taxis.

Ⓓ We saw Mayan pyramids and villages.

2. **Based on the information in Deanna's notes, which idea below is on topic and should be added to the notes?**

Ⓕ We saw a volcano near Mexico City.

Ⓖ We almost went to Canada instead.

Ⓗ Our family lives near Little Rock, Arkansas.

Ⓘ Mexico is located in North America.

3. **Based on the information in Deanna's notes, what kind of paper is she planning to write?**

Ⓐ A paper that gives information about Mexico

Ⓑ A paper that tells a story about a family trip

Ⓒ A paper that lists questions about Mexico

Ⓓ A paper that explains how to get to Mexico City

PRACTICE 2

Tyrone made the web below to organize ideas for a paper. Use his plan to answer questions 1–4.

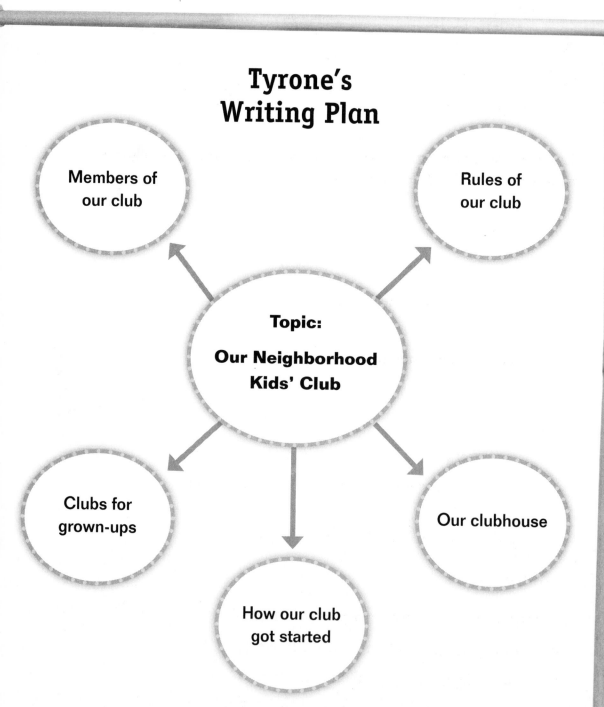

Tyrone's Writing Plan

Members of our club

Rules of our club

Topic:

Our Neighborhood Kids' Club

Clubs for grown-ups

Our clubhouse

How our club got started

Standardized Test Practice: Writing (Grades 3–4) © 2008 by Michael Priestley, Scholastic Teaching Resources

Name .... Date ....

1. **Which subtopic below is off topic and should be taken out of Tyrone's writing plan?**

Ⓐ Rules of our club

Ⓑ Clubs for grown-ups

Ⓒ How our club got started

Ⓓ Our clubhouse

2. **Based on the information in Tyrone's writing plan, which idea below is on topic and should be added to the plan?**

Ⓕ Clubs at school

Ⓖ Interesting hobbies for kids

Ⓗ Neighborhood families

Ⓘ Club meetings and activities

3. **Based on this writing plan, what kind of paper is Tyrone planning to write?**

Ⓐ A paper that tells an adventure story about a group of kids

Ⓑ A paper that describes a club for kids in his neighborhood

Ⓒ A paper that explains how to build a simple clubhouse

Ⓓ A paper that list tips for choosing the best club to join

4. **Tyrone wants to include this detail in his paper:**

Members of the club will meet every Sunday.

Under which subtopic does this detail belong?

Ⓕ Members of our club

Ⓖ How our club got started

Ⓗ Rules of our club

Ⓘ Our clubhouse

PRACTICE 3

Bethany is writing a paper about sharks and dolphins. She made the chart below to organize her ideas. Use her chart to answer questions 1–4.

	Sharks	Dolphins
Animal Group	fish	mammal
Habitat	oceans around the world may live near shores or in open seas	oceans around the world may live near shores or in open seas
Size	up to 40 feet long	up to 32 feet long
Appearance and Body Parts	long, sleek shape rough, scale-covered skin dorsal fin on back large tail fin with two parts	long, sleek shape smooth, rubbery skin dorsal fin on back pair of tail fins
Swimming	can swim very fast swim by moving tail fin back and forth	usually swim slowly swim by moving tail fins up and down
Characteristics	have gills for breathing can stay underwater all the time	have lungs for breathing must come to surface for air can be trained to perform

Standardized Test Practice: Writing (Grades 3–4) © 2008 by Michael Priestley, Scholastic Teaching Resources

Name .... Date ....

1. Based on the information in Bethany's chart, which idea below is on topic and should be added to the chart?

Ⓐ Dolphin training

Ⓑ Aquariums

Ⓒ Finding Food and Eating

Ⓓ Whales

2. Which detail about sharks should Bethany add to the chart under "Appearance and Body Parts"?

Ⓕ greatly feared by people

Ⓖ 360 different kinds of sharks

Ⓗ baby shark called a *pup*

Ⓙ have several rows of sharp teeth

3. Bethany wants to add this fact about dolphins to her chart:

communicate by making sounds

In which section of the chart should she write this fact?

Ⓐ Habitat

Ⓑ Size

Ⓒ Swimming

Ⓓ Characteristics

4. Based on the information in Bethany's chart, what kind of paper is she planning to write?

Ⓕ A paper that tells a story about a shark and a dolphin

Ⓖ A paper that describes how sharks and dolphins are alike and different

Ⓗ A paper that lists places where you can see dolphins perform

Ⓙ A paper that explains how people have harmed or helped sharks and dolphins

PRACTICE 4

Nick made this timeline to organize ideas for a paper. Use the timeline to answer questions 1–4.

Topic: Ben Franklin

1700

1706 Ben Franklin is born in Boston.

1716 Goes swimming in a pond.

1730 Marries Debbie Read.

1732 Publishes first *Poor Richard's Almanack*.

1746 Experiments with electricity.

1783 Helps form new government of the United States.

1790 Dies in Philadelphia.

1800

Standardized Test Practice: Writing (Grades 3–4) © 2008 by Michael Priestley, Scholastic Teaching Resources

Name .... Date ....

1. **Which event is unimportant and should be removed from the timeline?**

    Ⓐ   1706   Ben Franklin is born in Boston.

    Ⓑ   1716   Goes swimming in a pond.

    Ⓒ   1730   Marries Debbie Read.

    Ⓓ   1732   Publishes first *Poor Richard's Almanack*.

2. **Which of these events should be added to the timeline?**

    Ⓕ   1705   Father makes candles and soaps in Boston.

    Ⓖ   1707   Brother Samuel works as a blacksmith.

    Ⓗ   1720   Spends six pennies to see a lion in a cage.

    Ⓙ   1723   Moves to Philadelphia and becomes a printer.

3. **Which reference should Nick use to find more information about Ben Franklin?**

    Ⓐ   Encyclopedia

    Ⓑ   Dictionary

    Ⓒ   Newspaper

    Ⓓ   Almanac

4. **Based on the information in the timeline, what kind of paper does Nick plan to write?**

    Ⓕ   A story about how young Ben learned to swim

    Ⓖ   A paper explaining how electricity works

    Ⓗ   A report about Ben Franklin's life

    Ⓙ   A news article telling how Franklin invented a stove

Name .... Date ....

Maria wrote this profile of Shannon Boxx. Read the draft and think about ways to make it better. Then answer the questions.

A Soccer Superstar

(1) When the U.S. Women's Soccer Team played for the World Cup in 2007, one of the team's stars were Shannon Boxx. (2) It was Shannon's second World Cup experience. (3) She played soccer in high school and in college at Notre Dame. (4) In 2003, she tries out for the U.S. national team and made the squad. (5) At her first World Cup, she scored the team's first goal in a game against Sweden. (6) She also played in the Olympics in 2004. (7) Shannon scored the team's first goal in that tournament, too. (8) Today, Shannon Boxx is one of the world's best players.

1. **What change, if any, should be made in sentence 1?**

  Ⓐ Change *played* to *playing*.   Ⓒ Change *were* to *was*.

  Ⓑ Add a comma after *stars*.   Ⓓ Make no change.

2. **What sentence could *best* be added after sentence 2 to add more detail?**

  Ⓕ One of Shannon's teammates was Carli Lloyd.

  Ⓖ Shannon grew up in Redondo Beach, California.

  Ⓗ The United States has won two World Cups.

  Ⓙ Women's soccer has become very popular.

3. **What change, if any, should be made in sentence 4?**

  Ⓐ Change *tries* to *tried*.   Ⓒ Add a comma after *team*.

  Ⓑ Change *she* to *her*.   Ⓓ Make no change.

Standardized Test Practice: Writing (Grades 3–4) © 2008 by Michael Priestley, Scholastic Teaching Resources

Name .... Date ....

> Carla wrote this paper about tigers. Read Carla's paper and think about how she should correct and improve it. Then answer the questions.

Tigers Are Good News!

(1) Three months ago, animal lovers got great news. **(2)** The news came from a zoo in Buenos Aires, Argentina. **(3)** Three Bengal tiger cubs are born! **(4)** Two are female, and one is male. **(5)** All of the cubs are white. **(6)** This makes them extra special because white tigers are very rare.

(7) The white tiger cubs are healthy and playful, and they are growing fast. **(8)** At birth, the cubs weighed about two pounds. **(9)** In their first month, they each gained about 10 pounds. **(10)** One day, these animals may weigh nearly 600 pounds!

(11) Many people visit the zoo to see the tigers. **(12)** Visitors have fun thinking of names for the baby tigers, too. **(13)** Zoo officials have asked children to help give the cubs good names. **(14)** Thousands of children have put suggestions in a big box at the zoo.

1. **What change, if any, should be made in sentence 3?**

Ⓐ Insert *they* after *cubs.*   Ⓒ Change *born* to *borned.*

Ⓑ Change *are* to *were.*   Ⓓ Make no change.

2. **Which sentence could *best* be added after sentence 6?**

Ⓕ Most Bengal tigers are orange with black stripes.

Ⓖ Tigers are seen most often in India.

Ⓗ The zoo in Buenos Aires has many kinds of animals.

Ⓙ White rhinos are also very special.

3. **What change, if any, should be made in sentence 9?**

Ⓐ Change *their* to *its.*   Ⓒ Change *each* to *all.*

Ⓑ Change *they* to *he.*   Ⓓ Make no change.

Name .... Date ....

Read Josh's letter below. Then answer the questions that follow.

August 16

Dear Andrew,

Have you ever had a flat tire on your bike? That's what happened to me last weekend. I went riding with my cousin, Miguel. We were heading to Angel Falls for a picnic and a swim, and I thought I had planned the trip really well. We had lunches and bottles of water. We had hats and sunblock.

It was a nice day, and we whizzed down the road. Soon we were outside of town. We saw chipmunks and squirrels. Once we stopped to watch a big turtle cross the road.

Soon after we got back on our bikes, disaster struck! I must have ridden over a sharp rock, and my tire got softer and softer. I had a flat tire, but I didn't know what to do!

Luckily, Miguel came to the rescue. He had brought a tire patch kit. He knew how to patch my tire and showed me how to do it. Next time I go for a long ride, I might not bring lunch or sunblock. But I will bring a patch kit!

Your friend,
Josh

1. **Which is the *best* topic sentence to begin paragraph 2?**

Ⓐ   At first, we were having a great time.

Ⓑ   Miguel is a really cool guy.

Ⓒ   Here in Iowa, the weather varies a lot.

Ⓓ   I should have written to you sooner.

2. **What was the writer's purpose for writing this letter?**

Ⓐ   To explain how to fix a flat tire

Ⓑ   To describe the scenery near his home

Ⓒ   To tell a story about an adventure he had

Ⓓ   To give details about how to plan a bike trip

3. **Josh wants to add this sentence to the letter:**

I've learned my lesson.

Where is the *best* place to add this sentence?

Ⓐ   At the end of paragraph 1

Ⓑ   At the end of paragraph 2

Ⓒ   At the end of paragraph 3

Ⓓ   At the end of paragraph 4

Standardized Test Practice: Writing (Grades 3–4) © 2008 by Michael Priestley, Scholastic Teaching Resources

Name ....   Date ....

Read Javier's journal entry below. Then answer the questions that follow.

[1]   Today our class went on a field trip to a "living history museum." The museum is near Santa Fe, New Mexico, and has a Spanish name: El Rancho de las Golondrinas. That means "The Ranch of the Swallows." I know swallows are birds. I didn't see any swallows. I did see a lot of other interesting things.

[2]   We went through an old ranch house, a school, and a mill for grinding grain. We watched a woman make candles. She was dressed in clothes from long ago. Then we watched some men shear sheep. The sheep's wool was long and curly!

[3]   My favorite thing was watching the blacksmith. He worked over a hot, hot fire. It was fun to watch, but it looked like a hard job. It looked dangerous, too.

[4]   El Rancho is the best museum ever. It makes you feel like you are traveling back in time. It helps you understand how people lived long ago in New Mexico.

1. **What is the *best* way to combine these two sentences?**

   I didn't see any swallows. I did see a lot of other interesting things.

   Ⓐ   I didn't see any swallows, but I did see a lot of other interesting things.
   Ⓑ   I didn't see any swallows, or I did see a lot of other interesting things.
   Ⓒ   I didn't see any swallows, and I did see a lot of other interesting things.
   Ⓓ   I didn't see any swallows, I did see a lot of other interesting things.

2. **Which detail sentence could *best* be added to paragraph 3?**

   Ⓐ   Once I read a poem about a blacksmith.
   Ⓑ   It was right after lunch.
   Ⓒ   Sometimes we make campfires at my camp.
   Ⓓ   He was making horseshoes.

3. **Which is the *best* topic sentence to introduce the last paragraph?**

   Ⓐ   My sister thinks museums are kind of boring.
   Ⓑ   I learned a lot about New Mexico history today.
   Ⓒ   We had fun on the bus ride to El Rancho.
   Ⓓ   Last year I read an exciting book about time travel.

Name .... Date ....

Read Tonya's e-mail below. Then answer the questions that follow.

Date: April 1

To: <gram123@mail.com>

Hi, Grandma!

    Guess what! I'm going to be in a play at school. The play is really funny. It has three acts. Each act tells a funny story. The stories are new versions of old fairy tales that most people know. For example, "Little Red Riding Hood" and "The Three Bears." I got picked to play the part of Jackie in the story "Jackie and the Beanstalk." This story's ending is different from the one in "Jack and the Beanstalk." But I won't tell you how it ends. I hope you can come and see for yourself. The play is next Saturday at 2:00. Will you come? Let me know quick. The tickets are selling fast.

Love, Tonya

P.S. If you come, Mom said she will gladly pick you up at the train station. I hope you come I can't wait to see you!

---

1. **Which underlined word is *not* used correctly?**

  Ⓐ The play is <u>really</u> funny.

  Ⓑ Let me know <u>quick</u>.

  Ⓒ The tickets are selling <u>fast</u>.

  Ⓓ Mom said she will <u>gladly</u> pick you up at the train station.

2. **Which of these is *not* a complete sentence?**

  Ⓐ Guess what!

  Ⓑ For example, "Little Red Riding Hood" and "The Three Bears."

  Ⓒ But I won't tell you how it ends.

  Ⓓ Will you come?

3. **Which of these is a run-on sentence?**

  Ⓐ The stories are new versions of old fairy tales that most people know.

  Ⓑ This story's ending is different from the one in "Jack and the Beanstalk."

  Ⓒ I hope you can come and see for yourself.

  Ⓓ I hope you come I can't wait to see you!

Standardized Test Practice: Writing (Grades 3–4) © 2008 by Michael Priestley, Scholastic Teaching Resources

Name .... Date ....

Read Anna's how-to paper below. Then answer the questions that follow.

A New Room

Check out your bedroom. Is it time for a change? You can make big changes in a room just by moving the furniture. One thing I want is a new desk. A new arrangement can make a room feel new.

1. Find a pencil, a ruler, a tape measure, scissors, and some graph paper.

2. Measure the room and each piece of furniture. List the measurements.

3. Draw the outline of your room on graph paper. The squares on the paper make it easy. <u>If your wall is 10 feet long, draw a line that is 10 squares long</u>.

4. Draw each piece of furniture on the graph paper to get the correct size. Cut out each piece.

5. Get creative! This is the fun part. Arrange your paper furniture on your room plan. Try lots of arrangements. This furniture is light and easy to move!

6. When you're happy with your room plan, you'll be ready to move the *real* furniture.

   Now, enjoy your new room!

1. **Which is the *best* topic sentence to insert before the numbered steps?**

   Ⓐ I've been living in the same room all my life.

   Ⓑ Here are some tips for an easy and successful move.

   Ⓒ Nobody really needs a couch or sofa in a bedroom.

   Ⓓ Every student should have a quiet place for doing homework.

2. **Which sentence is off topic and should be removed from the first paragraph?**

   Ⓐ Check out your bedroom.

   Ⓑ You can make big changes in a room just by moving the furniture.

   Ⓒ One thing I want is a new desk.

   Ⓓ A new arrangement can make a room feel new.

3. **Which transition word or phrase should be added to the beginning of the underlined sentence to help connect it to the ideas in the paragraph?**

   Ⓐ For example,   Ⓒ As a result,

   Ⓑ Also,   Ⓓ Later on,

Here is the first draft of an informational paper. Use it to answer questions 1–4.

"Seeing" With Sound

(1) How do blind people get around safely? (2) Some people use special guide dogs. (3) A well-trained dog knows how to help its master cross busy streets and get from place to place. (4) Some people use long white canes to help them get around.

(5) Guide dogs and canes are helpful, but is there a better way for blind people to get around? (6) A scientist in England thought so. (7) He is a zoologist named Dean Waters which studies bats. (8) He knows that bats are able to fly in the dark without bumping into things. (9) Also, he knows that bats go by using sound to "see." (10) Dr. Waters wondered if people could do something similar.

(11) Bats as they fly make squeaking or clicking sounds. (12) These sounds travel outward in waves. (13) When the waves hit an object such as a tree or a house, they echo, or bounce back. (14) The waves travel back to the bat's ears. (15) From the echos, a bat learns the location and shape of objects around it. (16) This is called "echolocation."

(17) Dr. Waters talked to other scientists, including Deborah Withington and Brian Hoyle. (18) They all worked together and invented a new kind of cane. (19) At first they called it a "bat cane" because their idea started with bats. (20) The new cane has a computer in the handle. (21) It sends out high sounds that humans cannot hear. (22) The sound waves bounce off objects and echo back. (23) This causes buttons in the handle to buzz. (24) With a little training, a person using the cane can tell where objects are and can "see" with sound!

Standardized Test Practice: Writing (Grades 3–4) © 2008 by Michael Priestley, Scholastic Teaching Resources

Name .... Date ....

Standardized Test Practice: Writing (Grades 3–4) © 2008 by Michael Priestley, Scholastic Teaching Resources

1. **What change should be made in sentence 7?**

Ⓐ Capitalize *zoologist*.

Ⓑ Change *named* to *naming*.

Ⓒ Change *which* to *who*.

Ⓓ Change *studies* to *studys*.

2. **What word could replace the word *go* in sentence 9 to give the sentence more meaning?**

Ⓐ guide

Ⓑ drive

Ⓒ lead

Ⓓ navigate

3. **How can sentence 11 *best* be rewritten?**

Ⓐ As they fly squeaking or clicking, bats make sounds.

Ⓑ Bats make squeaking or clicking sounds as they fly.

Ⓒ As they fly, bats squeaking or clicking sounds make.

Ⓓ Bats make as they fly squeaking or clicking sounds.

4. **What change, if any, should be made in sentence 15?**

Ⓐ Change *echos* to *echoes*.

Ⓑ Change *learns* to *learned*.

Ⓒ Change *it* to *them*.

Ⓓ Make no change.

PRACTICE
12

Here is the first draft of a narrative that Patti wrote. It contains mistakes. Read the narrative to answer questions 1–4.

The Day My Tooth Got Knocked Out

[1] The day my tooth got knocked out started out like any other day. [2] I never dreamed when I got up that I would lose my front tooth forever.

[3] It happened in gym class when we were playing floor hockey with plastic hockey sticks. [4] As I was aiming my stick to slap the ball, I saw another girl with her stick high in the air. [5] The next second I felt a terrible pain on my mouth.

[6] I dropped my hockey stick and started crying because my mouth hurt so much. [7] The gym teacher was nice and brought me to the water fountain for a drink. [8] It was when I took a drink that I knew something bad had happened. [9] When the cold water hit the empty space where my tooth should have been, it hurt like crazy! [10] With my tongue I could feel that most of my front tooth was missing.

[11] I cried out that my tooth was gone. [12] The kids in my gym class heard and quickly got on the floor to look for my tooth. [13] Someone found it and gave it to me. [14] I walked to the nurse's office clutching my broken tooth in my hand and trying not to cry again.

[15] My dad came to the school to pick me up and take me to the dentist. [16] We live a few miles away from the school. [17] The dentist couldn't put the broken tooth back in. [18] He built a new tooth on top of what was left of my old tooth. [19] He made it out of some white paste that hardened when he shined a blue light on it. [20] Getting my new tooth took a long time.

[21] After a while, I stopped noticing my fake tooth. [22] It looks just like my old one. [23] Now I just have to be careful when I eat corn on the cob so it doesn't fall out again!

Standardized Test Practice: Writing (Grades 3–4) © 2008 by Michael Priestley, Scholastic Teaching Resources

Name .... Date ....

1. **The author wants to add this detail to the story.**

That girl had hit me with her hockey stick!

Which is the _best_ place to add this sentence to the story?

Ⓐ   After sentence 5

Ⓑ   After sentence 6

Ⓒ   After sentence 10

Ⓓ   After sentence 11

2. **Which sentence is unimportant to the story and should be removed?**

Ⓐ   Sentence 15

Ⓑ   Sentence 16

Ⓒ   Sentence 17

Ⓓ   Sentence 18

3. **The author wants to add a new paragraph to the story. Which information could be added between the fourth and fifth paragraphs to keep the story focused on the main idea?**

Ⓐ   Which team won the hockey game

Ⓑ   How the nurse helped the student

Ⓒ   What time the student went to bed

Ⓓ   What the dentist's office looked like

4. **What transition word should be added at the beginning of sentence 18 to connect it to the ideas in the fifth paragraph?**

Ⓐ   But

Ⓑ   Then

Ⓒ   Also

Ⓓ   So

Here is the first draft of a biographical paper that Tyler wrote. It has some mistakes. Read the paper to answer questions 1–4.

The Monkey Brigade

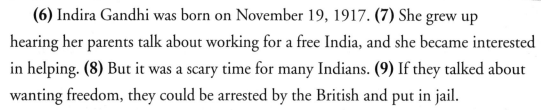

(1) The girl knew she had to be brave and think quickly. **(2)** If the soldiers discovered the secret papers, they would put many of her people in prison.

(3) This brave girl lived in India when it was ruled by England. **(4)** Many people of India wanted to run their own country and were trying hard to win India's freedom. **(5)** An example of those people was a girl, and she was named Indira Gandhi.

(6) Indira Gandhi was born on November 19, 1917. **(7)** She grew up hearing her parents talk about working for a free India, and she became interested in helping. **(8)** But it was a scary time for many Indians. **(9)** If they talked about wanting freedom, they could be arrested by the British and put in jail.

(10) When she was 12 years old, Indira formed a secret club called the Monkey Brigade. **(11)** The Monkey Brigade was made up of children like her. **(12)** Their main job was to learn secrets from the British about which people were to be arrested. **(13)** The children then warned those people. **(14)** They warned the people so soldiers could not arrest them. **(15)** The Monkey Brigade fooled the British because no one thought that children would help their country.

(16) Indira Gandhi knew her job as the leader of the Monkey Brigade was important. **(17)** One time she kept the British from finding secret papers hidden in the trunk of the car she was in. **(18)** The car was stopped by a British inspector who wanted to search it. **(19)** The man was very tall. **(20)** She begged him not to search the car because it would make her late for school. **(21)** The man believed her and let the car pass.

(22) Thanks to people like Indira Gandhi and her parents, India finally became free in 1947. **(23)** Twenty years later, Indira became the nation's prime minister.

Standardized Test Practice: Writing (Grades 3–4) © 2008 by Michael Priestley, Scholastic Teaching Resources

Name .... Date ....

1. What is the *best* way to revise sentence 5 so that it reads more clearly?

   Ⓐ One of those people was a girl named Indira Gandhi.

   Ⓑ An example of those people was named Indira Gandhi, a girl.

   Ⓒ One of those people was a girl and was named Indira Gandhi.

   Ⓓ A girl, she was named Indira Gandhi, was one of those people.

2. Which is the *best* way to combine sentences 13 and 14?

   Ⓕ The children then warned the soldiers so people could not arrest them.

   Ⓖ The children warned people, then so the soldiers could not arrest them.

   Ⓗ The children warned the people and the soldiers so they could not arrest them.

   Ⓙ The children then warned those people before soldiers could arrest them.

3. Which resource should the writer use to find more information about Indira Gandhi?

   Ⓐ Dictionary

   Ⓑ Encyclopedia

   Ⓒ Atlas

   Ⓓ Newspaper

4. Which sentence is unimportant to the passage and should be taken out?

   Ⓕ Sentence 17

   Ⓖ Sentence 18

   Ⓗ Sentence 19

   Ⓙ Sentence 20

Sam wrote the letter below to his new pen pal in Spain. The letter contains some mistakes. Read the letter to answer questions 1–4.

Dear Enzo,

(1) My name is Sam. **(2)** I live in Sterling, Vermont, in the United States. **(3)** I go to Sterling Elementary School, I'm in the third grade. **(4)** My teacher, Mrs. Green, is really nice. **(5)** We have an awesome playground at school, and we like to play capture the flag and kickball. **(6)** Do you have recess at your school?

(7) In my family, I have one sister named Emily. **(8)** We have a cat and a dog and a guinea pig as pets. **(9)** Our cat's name is Millie. **(10)** Our dog's name is Barkley. **(11)** Our guinea pig's name is Gary. **(12)** Gary eats lots of lettuce and carrots.

(13) My favorite class at school is gym. **(14)** We get to do cool stuff like jump rope and play lacrosse and ride scooters. **(15)** I like to play baseball and soccer. **(16)** I also like to ski and snowboard in the winter. **(17)** What sports do you play?

(18) I would like to hear about your school in Spain. **(19)** I hope I can go to Spain sometime. **(20)** My sister wants to go to Hawaii. **(21)** Do you have any brothers or sisters? **(22)** Do you like ice cream? **(23)** Write back soon.

Your friend,
Sam

Standardized Test Practice: Writing (Grades 3–4) © 2008 by Michael Priestley, Scholastic Teaching Resources

Name .... Date ....

1. **What change, if any, should be made in sentence 3?**

Ⓐ Change *School* to *school.*

Ⓑ Insert *and* after the comma.

Ⓒ Change *I'm* to *I'll.*

Ⓓ Make no change.

2. **Which sentence below *best* combines these sentences from the second paragraph?**

> We have a cat and a dog and a guinea pig as pets. Our cat's name is Millie. Our dog's name is Barkley. Our guinea pig's name is Gary.

Ⓕ Our cat and dog and guinea pig are named Millie, Barkley, and Gary.

Ⓖ Millie, Barkley, and Gary are the cat, dog, and guinea pig we have.

Ⓗ Our pets' names are Millie, Barkley, and Gary, and they are a cat, a dog, and a guinea pig.

Ⓙ We have a cat named Millie, a dog named Barkley, and a guinea pig named Gary.

3. **Which transition could *best* be added to connect sentence 15 to the rest of the paragraph?**

Ⓐ Also,

Ⓑ Therefore,

Ⓒ Then,

Ⓓ However,

4. **Which sentence is off topic and should be taken out of the letter?**

Ⓕ Sentence 18

Ⓖ Sentence 19

Ⓗ Sentence 20

Ⓙ Sentence 21

Standardized Test Practice: Writing (Grades 3–4) © 2008 by Michael Priestley, Scholastic Teaching Resources

Juanita wrote this draft of a news story for her school newspaper. The story has some mistakes. Read the story to answer questions 1–4.

Moose on the Loose

[1] People who live on Myrtle Street got a big surprise yesterday morning. [2] The surprise was more than six feet tall! [3] It had four legs and a huge set of antlers. [4] It was a moose that had wandered out of the woods.

[5] Sue Yi saw the moose first. [6] It was walking through her flower garden. [7] Ms. Yi called him on the telephone, and the moose headed into Joe Milano's yard. [8] The moose walked slowly across Mr. Milano's yard until it got to Max and Lea Burton's yard. [9] The Burtons' dog saw the moose and started barking loudly through an open window. [10] Mr. and Mrs. Burton looked out just in time to see the moose heading into the woods behind their house.

[11] The Burtons called their friend, Callie Howe. [12] She is a wildlife expert who teaches at the state college. [13] Ms. Howe explained, "Moose like to look for food in clearings and open areas. [14] They may wander into yards that are close to woods early in the morning, but usually you won't see them." [15] Ms. Howe also had some good advice for the Burtons and their neighbors. [16] "If you do see a moose," she said, "don't approach it or try to pet it. [17] Just let it go back to the woods where it wants to be."

Name .... Date ....

1. **What is the *best* way to write the underlined part of the sentence below?**

The surprise was more than six <u>feet</u> tall!

Ⓐ feets

Ⓑ foots

Ⓒ foot

Ⓓ Correct as is

2. **Juanita wants to add a topic sentence to the beginning of the second paragraph. Which of these would be the *best* topic sentence?**

Ⓕ Myrtle Street is a quiet street on the west side of town.

Ⓖ Four Myrtle Street neighbors spotted the moose in their backyards.

Ⓗ Deer have also been seen on Myrtle Street in the early evenings.

Ⓘ Myrtle Street is named after the myrtle trees that grow there.

3. **What is the *best* way to revise sentence 7?**

Ⓐ The moose headed into his yard when Ms. Yi called Joe Milano on the telephone.

Ⓑ Ms. Yi called Joe Milano and the moose headed into his yard on the telephone.

Ⓒ When the moose headed into Joe Milano's yard, Ms. Yi called Mr. Milano on the telephone.

Ⓓ On the telephone, Ms. Yi called the moose, and it headed into Joe Milano's yard.

4. **Juanita wants to replace the word *good* in sentence 15.**

Ms. Howe also had some *good* advice for the Burtons and their neighbors.

Which resource should Juanita use to find a more exact word for *good*?

Ⓕ An encyclopedia

Ⓖ A thesaurus

Ⓗ An almanac

Ⓘ A nature magazine

Marshall wrote this draft of a social studies report. It contains errors. Read the report to answer questions 1–4.

Tepees of the Great Plains Indians

(1) In North America, flat grasslands cover the middle of the continent. **(2)** They stretch all the way from Canada in the north to Texas in the south. **(3)** These grasslands are called the Great Plains. **(4)** For hundreds of years, American Indian tribes lived on the Great Plains. **(5)** There were about 30 different tribes in all. **(6)** The Sioux, Dakota, and Blackfoot were some of the most big tribes of the Great Plains.

(7) Each Great Plains tribe had its own language, customs, and traditions. **(8)** However, they were alike in an important way. **(9)** They lived in cone-shaped tents made from wooden poles covered with buffalo hides. **(10)** These shelters are called *tepees.*

(11) A tepee was a perfect shelter for Great Plains Indians. **(12)** Most of these tribes moved often from one campsite to another. **(13)** They traveled to hunt for buffalo or search for other food. **(14)** Some tribes also traveled to fight enemies. **(15)** A tepee was easy to put up or take down. **(16)** It could be wrapped up and hauled by a horse. **(17)** Spanish explorers brought horses to North America. **(18)** So when the Great Plains Indians were on the move, they took their tepees with them.

(19) The men found and cut down the tall, straight trees for the poles. **(20)** They also hunted buffalo for the tepee's hide cover. **(21)** This was a big job, since a dozen or more hides were needed for a cover. **(22)** Next, a group of women spent many days cleaning and softening the hides. **(23)** Then they spread the hides out to make a half-circle shape and sewed them together. **(24)** After that the women put the poles in place and arranged the cover over them. **(25)** When all this work was finally finished, the women enjoyed a feast prepared by the tepee's new owner.

Standardized Test Practice: Writing (Grades 3–4) © 2008 by Michael Priestley, Scholastic Teaching Resources

PRACTICE
·16·

Name .... Date ....

1. **What is the *best* way to write the underlined part of sentence 6?**

The Sioux, Dakota, and Blackfoot were some of the most big tribes of the Great Plains.

Ⓐ more big

Ⓑ biggest

Ⓒ most biggest

Ⓓ Correct as is

2. **Which sentence contains information that is unrelated to the report's main ideas?**

Ⓕ Sentence 4

Ⓖ Sentence 10

Ⓗ Sentence 17

Ⓘ Sentence 22

3. **Which of these is the *best* topic sentence to begin the fourth paragraph?**

Ⓐ When a family needed a tepee, the first step was hunting for buffalo.

Ⓑ The Great Plains Indians worked hard to survive.

Ⓒ The men and women of a tribe shared the job of making a tepee for a family.

Ⓓ A tepee had to be made to last for many years.

4. **To conclude this report, the writer should add a closing paragraph that —**

Ⓕ summarizes the most important ideas from the first four paragraphs.

Ⓖ tells more about the kinds of trees used for the poles of the tepees.

Ⓗ compares tepees to other kinds of houses and shelters.

Ⓘ adds more information about the customs of Great Plains tribes.

PRACTICE
17

Lawrence wrote this entry in his journal. He made some mistakes. Read the journal entry to answer questions 1–4.

(1) Every year on the night before school picture day, Grandma gets my best clothes ready. **(2)** She lays out my jacket and pants. **(3)** A white shirt and a tie. **(4)** "I spend good money for those pictures," she says, "and I want you to look handsome."

(5) I always cringe when I get dressed on picture day. **(6)** My classmates don't wear anything dressy for their pictures. **(7)** So I really stick out like a sore thumb. **(8)** When the other kids see me in my best clothes, they can be pretty mean.

(9) This year, the teasing bugged me more than ever. **(10)** Nolan Wilkie made fun of my clothes from the second I got on the bus. **(11)** I expected that from him, but even my friends laughed at me. **(12)** That bothered me a lot. **(13)** Then the lady who was taking the pictures made things worse. **(14)** When I sat on the stool, she whistled and said, "Young man, those are some fancy threads!"

(15) Nolan Wilkie howled and slapped his leg, and everyone else laughed, too. **(16)** The lady kept saying, "Big smile, now!" **(17)** How could I smile when I felt like yelling?

(18) We got our school pictures last week. **(19)** When I brang the package home, Grandma opened it right away. **(20)** "You look dreadful in these—and such a glum expression!" she exclaimed. **(21)** "I'm not going to pay for pictures like this."

(22) Then Grandma reached into the package and pulled out a slip of paper. **(23)** "Oh, that's a relief," she said after she read it. **(24)** "Retake day for school pictures is next Friday. **(25)** I'll have to lay out your best clothes the night before. **(26)** You'll remind me to do that, won't you, dear?"

(27) It's Thursday night, and Grandma has forgotten to lay out my best clothes. **(28)** In ten minutes, I'm supposed to turn off my light and go to bed. **(29)** What should I do?

Standardized Test Practice: Writing (Grades 3–4) © 2008 by Michael Priestley, Scholastic Teaching Resources

Name .... Date ....

1. **How can sentences 2 and 3 *best* be combined?**

   Ⓐ   She lays out my jacket, pants, a white shirt, and a tie.

   Ⓑ   She lays out my jacket, my pants, my white shirt, and my tie.

   Ⓒ   She lays out my jacket and pants, she lays out a white shirt and a tie.

   Ⓓ   With a white shirt and tie, she lays out my jacket and pants.

2. **Which sentence should be added after sentence 6 to support the ideas in the second paragraph?**

   Ⓕ   I wore my best clothes to my cousin's wedding.

   Ⓖ   They wear T-shirts, just like any other day.

   Ⓗ   My favorite jeans have holes in the knees.

   Ⓘ   Grandma's best dress has a lace collar.

3. **How should the underlined word in the sentence below be rewritten?**

   When I <u>brang</u> the package home, Grandma opened it right away.

   Ⓐ   bring

   Ⓑ   bringed

   Ⓒ   brought

   Ⓓ   Correct as is

4. **Which transition should be added to the beginning of sentence 27 to show the time order of events in the story?**

   Ⓕ   Now

   Ⓖ   Unless

   Ⓗ   Whenever

   Ⓘ   Also

Below is the first draft of a story that Heather wrote. The draft contains mistakes. Read the story to answer questions 1–4.

Something Under the Bed

(1) There was a big, old house at the end of Chestnut Lane. (2) No one had lived there for many years. (3) All the kids in the neighborhood thought the old house be haunted. (4) The kids never went near the house.

(5) One day some workers started fixing up the house. (6) They pulled off the rotted porch and built a new one. (7) They replaced the broken windows. (8) They fixed the crumbling chimney. (9) Their tools made a lot of noise. (10) They covered the faded gray paint with new, yellow paint.

(11) The work took many weeks. (12) When it was finally finished, a family moved into the house. (13) The family was made up of a mother, a father, and a boy named Jack. (14) He was ten years old.

(15) Before long, Jack made friends with Luis, a boy in the neighborhood. (16) Jack and Luis played together every day. (17) One day, Jack asked Luis to sleep over. (18) Without thinking, Luis said yes.

(19) The boys stayed up late that night. (20) They watched a scary movie on television. (21) Then they took turns telling spooky stories. (22) When they turned off the lights, Jack fell right to sleep, but Luis stayed awake. (23) Then he heard a strange sound coming from under his bed.

(24) Suddenly, Luis remembered that the house was haunted! (25) He jumped out of bed with a shout. (26) Just then, a creature scrambled out from under the bed. (27) It was Jack's dog, Sophie.

Standardized Test Practice: Writing (Grades 3–4) © 2008 by Michael Priestley, Scholastic Teaching Resources

Name .... Date ....

1. **What is the correct way to rewrite the underlined part of the sentence below?**

   All the kids in the neighborhood thought the old house <u>be</u> haunted.

   Ⓐ was

   Ⓑ were

   Ⓒ are

   Ⓓ Correct as is

2. **Which sentence contains a detail that is unimportant to the story?**

   Ⓕ Sentence 2

   Ⓖ Sentence 5

   Ⓗ Sentence 9

   Ⓙ Sentence 12

3. **Heather wants to add the following sentence to the fifth paragraph of the story:**

   It was the sound of breathing.

   Where should this be added to keep the events of the story in order?

   Ⓐ After sentence 19

   Ⓑ After sentence 21

   Ⓒ After sentence 22

   Ⓓ After sentence 23

4. **Heather wants to add a final paragraph to the story. Which event below should be added after the last paragraph to keep the story focused on the main idea?**

   Ⓕ Luis watching the workers fixing up the house

   Ⓖ Jack waking up and asking Luis why he shouted

   Ⓗ Luis meeting Jack for the first time

   Ⓙ Jack's parents unpacking their belongings when they move in

Below is the first draft of a book report that Lucy wrote. The draft contains mistakes. Read the report to answer questions 1–4.

A Sand Fairy Makes Mischief

(1) Suppose a magical creature offers to make you're wishes come true. (2) You think up a wonderful wish and tell the creature what you want. (3) The wish comes true, too, but in an unexpected way. (4) That's exactly what happens to the children in *Five Children and It*. (5) A fantasy novel by Edith Nesbit.

(6) The five young children in this story are three brothers and two sisters. (7) They live in a large, old house in the countryside of England. (8) One day, when the children are digging in a gravel pit, they uncover an ancient sand fairy. (9) It is a small, ugly creature covered with fur. (10) Although the sand fairy is grouchy and impatient, it promises to grant the children one wish a day.

(11) On the first day, the children wish to be beautiful. (12) Next, they wish to become rich. (13) On another day, they wish to grow wings and fly. (14) Before long, they start getting carried away with their wishes. (15) They even wish to turn their house into a castle surrounded by unfriendly knights. (16) The cranky sand fairy is full of mischief. (17) It grants each wish with a sly twist that always causes some unpleasant trouble for the children.

(18) The children in *Five Children and It* don't have much fun when their wishes go terribly wrong. (19) However, the story's constant surprises make it fun to read.

Standardized Test Practice: Writing (Grades 3–4) © 2008 by Michael Priestley, Scholastic Teaching Resources

Name .... Date ....

1. **What is the correct way to write the underlined part of the sentence below?**

Suppose a magical creature offers to make <u>you're</u> wish come true.

(A) yours

(B) your

(C) you

(D) Correct as is

2. **What is the *best* way to revise sentences 4 and 5?**

(F) That's exactly what happens to the children in *Five Children and It,* a fantasy novel by Edith Nesbit.

(G) That's exactly what happens in a novel by Edith Nesbit, *Five Children and It,* a fantasy novel.

(H) That's exactly what happens in the fantasy novel by Edith Nesbit. *Five Children and It.*

(J) Best as it is

3. **Lucy wants to add the following sentence to the second paragraph:**

It has the eyes of a snail, the hands and feet of a monkey, and the ears of a bat.

Where should this detail be added to organize the ideas correctly?

(A) After sentence 7

(B) After sentence 8

(C) After sentence 9

(D) After sentence 10

4. **Which of these sentences best fits in the conclusion of this book report?**

(F) When you finish the book, you can watch the movie on DVD.

(G) There are lots of other great books with fairy characters, too.

(H) Some young people would rather read mysteries or science fiction.

(J) If you enjoy fantasy that's both fun and exciting, you should read this book.

Standardized Test Practice: Writing (Grades 3–4) © 2008 by Michael Priestley, Scholastic Teaching Resources

Remi wrote the letter below to his Aunt Mitra. The letter has some mistakes. Read the letter to answer questions 1–4.

1418 Peach Blossom Lane

Atlanta, GA 30327

April 30

Dear Aunt Mitra,

[1] I really enjoyed your visit here last month. [2] My favorite part of your visit was making the beautiful butterfly kite with you. [3] As it turns out, that kite led to quite an adventure for Mom and me.

[4] The adventure started when I brought the butterfly kite to school. [5] My classmates really liked it. [6] Some of them even asked me to make kites for them. [7] Then my teacher, Mr. Humphrey, said, "You should make kites to sell at the school craft fair on Saturday!"

[8] I planned to make one kite every night. [9] So I made one on Monday night and another on Tuesday night. [10] Something unexpected happened. [11] At soccer practice on Wednesday, I fell and badly sprained my wrist. [12] The injury pushed the kites right out of my head for two days. [13] On Friday night, I remembered I still had three kites to make. [14] With my wrist and hand wrapped in a stiff bandage, that was a problem!

[15] Luckily, Mom came to my rescue. [16] We sat down together with the kite materials. [17] I gave her directions, and she followed them, step by step. [18] When Mom finished the last kite, it was almost midnight. [19] There was a full moon, but it was too cloudy to see it. [20] Mom and I were tired but very relieved when we finally went to bed.

[21] I hope this story gave you a laugh. [22] Mom and I can't wait to see you again. [23] Maybe this summer we can drive to your house for a visit.

Your favorite nephew,

Remi

Standardized Test Practice: Writing (Grades 3–4) © 2008 by Michael Priestley, Scholastic Teaching Resources

Name .... Date ....

1. **Which sentence below should be added to support the ideas in the second paragraph?**

   Ⓐ I quickly promised to make five kites.

   Ⓑ Last year I bought some neat clay figures at the crafts fair.

   Ⓒ Mr. Humphrey is one of the best teachers I've ever had.

   Ⓓ The crafts fair is held in our school's all-purpose room.

2. **Remi wants to add the following sentence to the letter:**

   We have sharing time every Monday, and I wanted to show off the kite.

   Where should this detail be added to organize the ideas correctly?

   Ⓕ After sentence 2

   Ⓖ After sentence 4

   Ⓗ After sentence 7

   Ⓙ After sentence 8

3. **Which transition should be added to the beginning of sentence 10 to help connect the ideas in the paragraph?**

   Ⓐ Usually

   Ⓑ Besides

   Ⓒ Then

   Ⓓ Also

4. **Which sentence is off topic and should be taken out of the fourth paragraph?**

   Ⓕ Sentence 15

   Ⓖ Sentence 17

   Ⓗ Sentence 19

   Ⓙ Sentence 20

Emmett wrote this draft of a paper to tell his class about a special event in history. Read Emmett's paper and think about how he should correct and improve it. Then answer the questions.

To the Rescue!

(1) During a storm in 1896, a ship ran aground off the North Carolina coast. **(2)** Huge waves began to break it up. **(3)** The passengers feared for there lives. **(4)** On shore, the men of Pea Island Life-Saving Station 17 had spotted the ship. **(5)** But they could not use their surfboat for a rescue because the sea was too wild. **(6)** Station 17's captain said, "Men, we must try to swim to the ship."

(7) The two strongest swimmers being joined together by a rope. **(8)** Another man on shore held the rope's end. **(9)** The two men dove into the waves and swam out to the broken ship. **(10)** It took nine trips to save them all.

(11) The U.S. Life-Saving Service began in 1871, in the days of sailing ships. **(12)** Along the Atlantic coast, crews lived and worked in station houses. **(13)** They walked the beach night and day, looking for ships in trouble. **(14)** Some people like to collect shells on the beach. **(15)** If they spotted one, they sent up a flare. **(16)** That told the ship that help was on the way.

(17) Station 17 was the only one in the Life-Saving Service with an African-American crew. **(18)** Like their captain, Richard Etheridge, many of the men had been born as slaves. **(19)** All had grown up on Pea Island and were used to being out on the water year round.

(20) By the 1930s, the stations were no longer needed. **(21)** Station 17 closed in 1947. **(22)** In 1992, the Coast Guard finally honored the members of this crew for their daring rescue almost 100 years before.

Standardized Test Practice: Writing (Grades 3–4) © 2008 by Michael Priestley, Scholastic Teaching Resources

Name .... Date ....

1. **What change, if any, should be made in sentence 3?**

   Ⓐ   Change *passengers* to *passagers*.

   Ⓑ   Insert *were* before *feared*.

   Ⓒ   Change *there* to *their*.

   Ⓓ   Make no change.

2. **What change, if any, should be made in sentence 7?**

   Ⓕ   Change *strongest* to *most strong*.

   Ⓖ   Capitalize *swimmers*.

   Ⓗ   Change *being* to *were*.

   Ⓙ   Make no change.

3. **Which sentence could *best* be added after sentence 9?**

   Ⓐ   There are many dangerous places along the coast.

   Ⓑ   Ships often hit the reefs near the North Carolina shore.

   Ⓒ   Members of the crew also had to know first aid.

   Ⓓ   One by one, the passengers were carried safely to shore.

4. **Which sentence does *not* belong in this paper?**

   Ⓕ   Sentence 11

   Ⓖ   Sentence 14

   Ⓗ   Sentence 17

   Ⓙ   Sentence 20

Meredith wrote this draft of a how-to paper. It has some errors. Read the paper to answer questions 1–4.

How to Make Sidewalk Chalk

1 Did you know you can make your own chalk for drawing on the sidewalk? **2** It's really very easy. **3** You end up with much brighter colors than you can buy. **4** All you need is plaster of Paris, poster paints, and something to mold the chalk in. **5** Hardware stores and art supply stores for the first two. **6** Poster paint is sold in packs of little bottles. **7** Each bottle holds a few tablespoons of paint.

8 For molds, you can use small paper cups. **9** The kind of cups that go in a bathroom dispenser are good. **10** My friend Karen likes to draw pictures with chalk. **11** Cardboard toilet paper holders with foil over one end also work.

12 To begin, cover your work surface with newspaper. **13** Then, in a plastic bowl, mix 1 cup of plaster of Paris with 1/2 cup of water. **14** Use a plastic spoon or wooden Popsicle stick to stir. **15** Be sure to mix in all the dry plaster in the corners. **16** Add 2 to 3 tablespoons of poster paint and mix until no streaks of color show.

17 Pour the mixture into the molds. **18** Tap each one gently on the counter. **19** This makes any air bubbles rise to the top.

20 For more colors, mix different paints. **21** White paint added to red makes pink, and blue and yellow make green.

22 Set the molds on newspapers to dry. **23** In less than 24 hours, your brightly colored chalk will be ready to use.

Standardized Test Practice: Writing (Grades 3–4) © 2008 by Michael Priestley, Scholastic Teaching Resources

Name .... Date ....

1. **Which is the *best* way to combine sentences 2 and 3?**

Ⓐ   It's really very easy, if you end up with much brighter colors than you can buy.

Ⓑ   It's really very easy, and you end up with much brighter colors than you can buy.

Ⓒ   It's really very easy, but you end up with much brighter colors than you can buy.

Ⓓ   It's really very easy, therefore you end up with much brighter colors than you can buy.

2. **Which of these is *not* a complete sentence and should be corrected?**

Ⓐ   **4** All you need is plaster of Paris, poster paints, and something to mold the chalk in.

Ⓑ   **5** Hardware stores and art supply stores for the first two.

Ⓒ   **6** Poster paint is sold in packs of little bottles.

Ⓓ   **7** Each bottle holds a few tablespoons of paint.

3. **Which sentence is off topic and should be taken out of this paper?**

Ⓐ   Sentence 8

Ⓑ   Sentence 9

Ⓒ   Sentence 10

Ⓓ   Sentence 11

4. **Which transition word or phrase should be added to the beginning of sentence 21?**

Ⓐ   For example,

Ⓑ   Meanwhile,

Ⓒ   As a result,

Ⓓ   Further,

Glenn wrote this draft of a personal narrative. It has some mistakes. Read the narrative to answer questions 1–8.

The Sketch Artist

(1) When I was nine years old, my mom taught a class for any kids in the neighborhood who wanted to try drawing. (2) At least ten of us sat around a table in our basement with paper and pencils. (3) I liked it, and after a while I felt like I was really learning to draw.

(4) One of the first things she taught us was how to make a contour drawing. (5) This involves making rough shapes to show the basic form of whatever you are drawing. (6) She trained us for this kind of drawing to work quick. (7) In contour drawings, we sometimes drew balloons for body parts. (8) We'd make long skinny balloons for arms and legs, a rough triangle for the shoulders and chest, and an oval for the head.

(9) In the third and fourth weeks, Mom showed us how to do a quick face sketch. (10) Drawing faces was fun. (11) We would draw an oval for a face. (12) Then, with a few lines, we'd make the face actually look like someone. (13) This was my favoritest part of the class, even though I didn't think I would ever have to use this skill.

(14) One afternoon in August, something unusual happened. (15) I was walking into a convenience store to buy a cold drink. (16) As I reached for the door, it opened fast, and out came a young man carrying a paper bag. (17) Ran right past me, jumped into a car, and sped away. (18) Two minutes later, a police car screeched into the parking lot.

(19) As I soon found out, the young man who ran past me was a thief. (20) He had just stolen some things from the store. (21) I was standing there. (22) The police asked me for a description of the young man. (23) I couldn't describe him very well, and the police kept asking for more details. (24) Then I suddenly got an idea. (25) I could make a sketch of the man's face! (26) So that's what I did the police caught him a few hours later.

(27) The store owner gave me a small reward for helping the police. (28) He also said I could have a free cold drink any time I wanted for the rest of the summer.

Standardized Test Practice: Writing (Grades 3–4) © 2008 by Michael Priestley, Scholastic Teaching Resources

Name .... Date ....

Standardized Test Practice: Writing (Grades 3–4) © 2008 by Michael Priestley, Scholastic Teaching Resources

1. Which sentence can *best* be added to the first paragraph?

   Ⓐ Some drawings were really good.

   Ⓑ We met once a week all summer.

   Ⓒ Two of my friends are good artists.

   Ⓓ I can't figure out how to draw feet.

2. What change, if any, should be made in sentence 4?

   Ⓕ Change *teached* to *taught*.

   Ⓖ Change *was* to *were*.

   Ⓗ Change *us* to *we*.

   Ⓙ Make no change.

3. What is the *best* way to revise sentence 6?

   Ⓐ To work quick, she trained us for this kind of drawing.

   Ⓑ She trained us quick for this kind of drawing to work.

   Ⓒ For this kind of drawing, she trained us to work quick.

   Ⓓ She trained us to work quickly for this kind of drawing.

4. What change, if any, should be made in sentence 13?

   Ⓕ Change *This* to *These*.

   Ⓖ Change *favoritest* to *favorite*.

   Ⓗ Change even *though* to *because*.

   Ⓙ Make no change.

5. **Which of these is an incomplete sentence and should be revised?**

Ⓐ   Sentence 14

Ⓑ   Sentence 15

Ⓒ   Sentence 17

Ⓓ   Sentence 18

6. **What is the *best* way to combine sentences 21 and 22?**

Ⓕ   I was standing there, but the police asked me for a description of the young man.

Ⓖ   Before I was standing there, the police asked me for a description of the young man.

Ⓗ   I was standing there, because the police asked me for a description of the young man.

Ⓙ   Since I was standing there, the police asked me for a description of the young man.

7. **What is the *best* way to rewrite sentence 26?**

Ⓐ   So that's what I did, but the police caught him a few hours later.

Ⓑ   So that's what I did, and the police caught him a few hours later.

Ⓒ   So that's what the police did, and I caught him a few hours later.

Ⓓ   Best as it is

8. **What change, if any, should be made in sentence 27?**

Ⓕ   Change *gave* to *gives*.

Ⓖ   Change *helping* to *help*.

Ⓗ   Insert a comma after *reward*.

Ⓙ   Make no change.

Standardized Test Practice: Writing (Grades 3–4) © 2008 by Michael Priestley, Scholastic Teaching Resources

Jennifer wrote this draft of a news story. It contains mistakes. Read the news story to answer questions 1–8.

The Garbage Patch

(1) Way out in the middle of the Pacific Ocean, there is a place known as "the garbage patch." **(2)** This patch is made up of fishnets, plastic, and other trash that collects in one place. **(3)** The Pacific garbage patch is twice the size of Texas. **(4)** Texas is a very big state!

(5) How did all this trash get into the ocean. **(6)** Most of it comes from the land. **(7)** Wind blows trash off of open dumps in Mexico. **(8)** Storm water washes litter from California streets into rivers, and rivers carry it into the ocean. **(9)** Fishing boats lose their nets. **(10)** Some ships dump their garbage in the ocean, even though it's against the law. **(11)** One ship from Asia is called *Pacific Queen*.

(12) Shipping containers fall overboard. **(13)** This might happen in a storm or by accident. **(14)** For example, in 1992, a container of plastic toy ducks fell off a Chinese ship in the Pacific. **(15)** In 2003, large numbers of the toy ducks washed up on beaches in Europe. **(16)** People don't get away from their trash by dumping it in the ocean. **(17)** Sooner or later, it shows up somewhere.

(18) The trash in the Pacific garbage patch harms animals and the environment. **(19)** Young seals get caught in old fishing nets. **(20)** Birds eat the plastic trash, thinking it is food. **(21)** Trash sometimes washes ashore on beaches. **(22)** Already trash has covered the beaches in parts of Hawaii.

(23) Someone has to start cleaning up all this trash. **(24)** One group of concerned people is working on it. **(25)** They pull garbage out of the patch and burn them. **(26)** But more collects there every day.

(27) The U.S. government has decided to start helping, too. **(28)** A law passed recently will put $15 million into clean-up efforts.

Name .... Date ....

1. **What is the *best* way to combine sentences 3 and 4?**

Ⓐ   Since the Pacific garbage patch is twice the size of Texas, Texas is a very big state!

Ⓑ   The Pacific garbage patch is twice the size of Texas, although Texas is a very big state!

Ⓒ   The Pacific garbage patch is twice the size of Texas, and Texas is a very big state!

Ⓓ   While the Pacific garbage patch is twice the size of Texas, Texas is a very big state!

2. **What change, if any, should be made in sentence 5?**

Ⓕ   Change *How* to *Where*.

Ⓖ   Change *did* to *does*.

Ⓗ   Change the period to a question mark.

Ⓙ   Make no change.

3. **Which sentence can *best* be added after sentence 8 to help organize ideas in the second paragraph?**

Ⓐ   The rest of the trash comes from ships.

Ⓑ   It's hard to say why people create trash.

Ⓒ   California has more people than any other state.

Ⓓ   Even young children know they should not litter.

4. **Which sentence contains an unimportant detail and should be removed from the passage?**

Ⓕ   Sentence 9

Ⓖ   Sentence 10

Ⓗ   Sentence 11

Ⓙ   Sentence 12

5. What transition word or phrase should be added to the beginning of sentence 12?

Ⓐ In a way,

Ⓑ Sometimes,

Ⓒ On the other hand,

Ⓓ As a matter of fact,

6. The writer wants to add this detail sentence to the news story.

The birds cannot digest plastic, and eventually they die.

Where does this sentence fit best?

Ⓕ After sentence 18

Ⓖ After sentence 20

Ⓗ After sentence 21

Ⓙ After sentence 22

7. Which is the *best* way to revise sentence 25?

Ⓐ They pull garbages out of the patch and burn them.

Ⓑ They burn garbage when they pull it out of the patch.

Ⓒ They pull out garbage of the patch and burn them.

Ⓓ They pull garbage out of the patch and burn it.

8. Which sentence can *best* be added as a concluding sentence at the end of the last paragraph?

Ⓕ Help is finally coming, and not a moment too soon.

Ⓖ The U.S. government spends a lot of money every year.

Ⓗ I doubt that anyone can solve this problem.

Ⓙ People should stop dumping their trash in the ocean.

Hannah wrote this draft of a biographical paper. It contains errors. Read the biography to answer questions 1–8.

The School Builder

(1) In 1993, Greg Mortenson tried to climb a mountain called K2 in Pakistan. **(2)** His attempt was a failure. **(3)** First, he never reached the top. **(4)** Then he got lost on his way back down. **(5)** He finally stumbled into a small mountain village named Korphe. **(6)** He was starving and sick. **(7)** The people of Korphe fed him and helped him recover.

(8) Greg had been in poor places before. **(9)** But he was amazed to see how poor these villagers were. **(10)** They had no paper or pencils. **(11)** Children used the frozen ground for a chalkboard. **(12)** The village couldn't not afford to pay a dollar a day for a teacher. **(13)** Before he left, Mortenson promised that someday he would build them a school.

(14) When he got back to America, Greg worked as a nurse in a hospital. **(15)** To save money, he lived in his car. **(16)** He sent almost 600 letters to famous rich people, asking them to help build a school for Korphe. **(17)** For months, he got no reply's. **(18)** Then one day he got a check for $12,000! **(19)** With the money he had saved from working, he had enough to start building.

(20) Even before he got back to Korphe, Greg faced many dangers. **(21)** He had to drive his truck along dangerous mountain roads. **(22)** With one wrong move, he'd be over a cliff.

(23) Greg had to learn some things, too. **(24)** He was in a hurry before winter to get the school built. **(25)** Village life moves slowly. **(26)** At first, the villagers was patient with him, but he kept pushing. **(27)** Then someone told him, "These mountains have been here a long time, and so have we. **(28)** You might as well slow down because we are in no rush."

(29) Finally, after three years of raising money and building, Korphe had a school.

(30) Greg has built more than 50 schools in northern Pakistan. **(31)** Some people do not agree with his views or support his efforts. **(32)** But Greg Mortenson keeps on doing what he knows is right: helping poor children build a better future.

Standardized Test Practice: Writing (Grades 3–4) © 2008 by Michael Priestley, Scholastic Teaching Resources

Name .... Date ....

1. **What is the *best* way to combine sentences 5 and 6?**

Ⓐ He finally stumbled into a small mountain village named Korphe, and he was starving and sick.

Ⓑ Starving and sick, named Korphe, he finally stumbled into a small mountain village.

Ⓒ He finally stumbled into a small mountain village, starving and sick, named Korphe.

Ⓓ When he finally stumbled into a small mountain village named Korphe, he was starving and sick.

2. **Which sentence below should be added after sentence 8 to support the ideas in the second paragraph?**

Ⓕ He had grown up in Africa, where his parents were missionaries.

Ⓖ Greg felt that he might be in danger.

Ⓗ The children of the village did not know what fractions were.

Ⓙ He couldn't wait to leave the village.

3. **What change, if any, should be made in sentence 12?**

Ⓐ Change *couldn't* to *could'nt*.

Ⓑ Delete the word *not*.

Ⓒ Change *to pay* to *paying*.

Ⓓ Make no change.

4. **How should sentence 17 be rewritten?**

Ⓕ For months, he got no replies.

Ⓖ For months he got no replys.

Ⓗ For months, he didn't get no reply's.

Ⓙ Best as it is

5. The writer wants to add the following sentence to the third paragraph:

He began to lose hope.

Where should this sentence be added to organize the ideas correctly?

Ⓐ   After sentence 16

Ⓑ   After sentence 17

Ⓒ   After sentence 18

Ⓓ   After sentence 19

6. **How should sentence 24 be rewritten?**

Ⓕ   To get the school built, he was in a hurry before winter.

Ⓖ   Before winter, he was in a hurry to get the school built.

Ⓗ   He was in a hurry to get the school built before winter.

Ⓙ   Best as it is

7. **What change, if any, should be made in sentence 26?**

Ⓐ   Remove the comma after *him.*

Ⓑ   Change *patient* to *patent.*

Ⓒ   Change *was* to *were.*

Ⓓ   Make no change.

8. **What transition word or phrase should be added to the beginning of sentence 30 to connect it to the previous paragraph?**

Ⓕ   As a result,

Ⓖ   Since then,

Ⓗ   However,

Ⓙ   For example,

Standardized Test Practice: Writing (Grades 3–4) © 2008 by Michael Priestley, Scholastic Teaching Resources

Zeke wrote this draft of a personal essay. It contains some errors. Read the essay to answer questions 1–8.

My Favorite Way to See a Movie

(1) Ever since I was really little, I have loved movies. **(2)** They take me to places I can't go on my own. **(3)** They make me laugh and cry. **(4)** They show how it feels to be another person who lives in a place I'll probably never go to. **(5)** When anyone asks me, "Do you want to see a movie?" I always say, "Sure!"

(6) Sometimes I watch movies at home, and sometimes I go to a theater. **(7)** At home I can watch movies with a video or DVD player. **(8)** When you watch a movie at home, no one throws popcorn at you or says you're making too much noise. **(9)** Also, you can watch the movie whenever you want. **(10)** Another thing is you can stop the movie whenever you need to.

(11) My mom or my stepdad usually take me to the library on weekends. **(12)** I can pick out four movies at a time. **(13)** That's how I found *Porco Rosso*, one of my favorite animated movies. **(14)** It's about a man who is half pig and flies planes over the Mediterranean Sea. **(15)** He fights other planes in the air. **(16)** The flying scenes are good. **(17)** I would never have seen this movie in a theater because it came out before I was born.

(18) Sometimes I invite friends to my house to watch with me. **(19)** Then it doesn't matter if they don't have enough money to go to a theater.

(20) One problem with watching movies on DVD is that you have to wait until they leave the theater to see them. **(21)** Also, the screen is small compared to the one in a movie theater. **(22)** Sometimes the biggest screen is better. **(23)** I'm glad I saw *Charlotte's Web* in a theater. **(24)** It seemed more magical that way. **(25)** When the lights came up, everyone was really quiet but smiling. **(26)** Many people had tears in their eyes.

(27) Sometimes it's best to see a movie in a big, dark place with a bunch of strangers. **(28)** In general, though, I'd rather watch movies at home than watch them in a theater.

Name .... Date ....

1. **Which sentence *best* states the main idea of this essay?**

    Ⓐ When anyone asks me, "Do you want to see a movie?"
        I always say, "Sure!"

    Ⓑ Sometimes it's best to see a movie in a big, dark place with
        a bunch of strangers.

    Ⓒ In general, though, I'd rather watch movies at home than
        watch them in a theater.

    Ⓓ Ever since I was really little, I have loved movies.

2. **In the first paragraph, which sentence repeats something that
    has already been stated?**

    Ⓕ Sentence 1

    Ⓖ Sentence 3

    Ⓗ Sentence 4

    Ⓙ Sentence 5

3. **What change, if any, should be made in sentence 11?**

    Ⓐ Capitalize *mom.*

    Ⓑ Change *take* to *takes.*

    Ⓒ Change *me* to *I.*

    Ⓓ Make no change.

4. **What change, if any, should be made in sentence 14?**

    Ⓕ Change *It's* to *Its.*

    Ⓖ Change *who* to *which.*

    Ⓗ Change *Sea* to *sea.*

    Ⓙ Make no change.

Standardized Test Practice: Writing (Grades 3–4) © 2008 by Michael Priestley, Scholastic Teaching Resources

5. The writer wants to use a different word for *good* in the sentence below to make the sentence more descriptive.

> The flying scenes are good.

Which word would fit *best* in this sentence?

Ⓐ attractive

Ⓑ breathtaking

Ⓒ happy

Ⓓ funny

6. **Which sentence would *best* support the ideas in the fourth paragraph?**

Ⓕ Some of my friends can't afford to buy a movie ticket.

Ⓖ I'm not too fond of the scary parts.

Ⓗ I usually do my homework before I watch a movie.

Ⓙ Theaters have more comfortable chairs.

7. **What transition word or phrase should be added to the beginning of sentence 20 to introduce the ideas in the fifth paragraph?**

Ⓐ Likewise,

Ⓑ Instead,

Ⓒ On the other hand,

Ⓓ Also,

8. **How should sentence 22 be rewritten?**

Ⓕ Sometimes the biggest screen is more good.

Ⓖ Sometimes the bigger screen is gooder.

Ⓗ Sometimes the bigger screen is more better.

Ⓙ Sometimes the bigger screen is better.

Name .... Date ....

> Read the article "Miniature Golf." Choose the word or words that correctly fit in each blank for questions 1–4.

Miniature Golf

Have you ever played miniature __(1)__ It is lots of fun. Mini-golf is played on a very small course. You use only one club, called a "putter," to hit a golf ball into a hole. Most courses have 18 holes, and each of the holes __(2)__ different. You have to hit the golf ball around trees, little ponds, and other obstacles to get to the hole. Some mini-golf courses have windmills, clowns, and other goofy things. Some courses are __(3)__ like theme parks and have names like Pirate's Cove or Black Mountain. If you haven't played mini-golf yet, you should try __(4)__ soon.

1. **Which answer goes in blank 1?**

Ⓐ golf,

Ⓑ golf?

Ⓒ golf.

Ⓓ golf!

2. **Which answer goes in blank 2?**

Ⓐ is

Ⓑ are

Ⓒ be

Ⓓ were

3. **Which answer goes in blank 3?**

Ⓐ builded

Ⓑ building

Ⓒ built

Ⓓ builds

4. **Which answer goes in blank 4?**

Ⓐ them

Ⓑ us

Ⓒ him

Ⓓ it

Standardized Test Practice: Writing (Grades 3–4) © 2008 by Michael Priestley, Scholastic Teaching Resources

Name .... Date ....

> **Read the letter from Sandra. Choose the word or words that correctly fit in each blank for questions 5–8.**

August 10

Dear ___(5)___

My brother and I are taking a long train trip. We started in ___(6)___.
This morning we rode through the Adirondack Mountains. Right
now, we are on our way to Niagara Falls. We will stop there for a
couple of hours. I ___(7)___ wait to see the waterfalls. After that, we will
travel west. In about three days, we ___(8)___ in California.

I'll send you a postcard when we get there!

Love,
Sandra

5. **Which answer goes in blank 5?**

Ⓐ Aunt polly:

Ⓑ aunt Polly,

Ⓒ Aunt Polly,

Ⓓ Aunt Polly.

6. **Which answer goes in blank 6?**

Ⓐ Port henry, New york

Ⓑ Port Henry, New York

Ⓒ port Henry, New York

Ⓓ Port Henry New York

7. **Which answer goes in blank 7?**

Ⓐ can hardly

Ⓑ cannot hardly

Ⓒ can't hardly

Ⓓ can't not hardly

8. **Which answer goes in blank 8?**

Ⓐ are

Ⓑ were

Ⓒ being

Ⓓ will be

PRACTICE 27

Editing Practice A

For questions 9–16, choose the best answer to each question.

9. Which is a complete sentence?

(A) Mr. Churchill's class.

(B) Going on a field trip today.

(C) The Gold Rush Museum.

(D) We'll be back at 3:00.

10. Read the following sentence:

Most kinds of flies have one pair of wings, because bees and wasps have two.

What is the correct way to rewrite the sentence?

(A) Most kinds of flies have one pair of wings, so bees and wasps have two.

(B) Most kinds of flies have one pair of wings, but bees and wasps have two.

(C) Most kinds of flies have one pair of wings, or bees and wasps have two.

(D) Leave as is.

11. Which sentence below is written correctly?

(A) "Wait for me!" cried the little boy.

(B) "Wait for me! cried the little boy."

(C) "Wait for me" cried the little boy!

(D) Wait for me! "cried the little boy."

12. In the sentence below, what is the subject?

Last week, Grandpa Leo sent me a birthday present.

(A) week   (C) me

(B) Grandpa Leo   (D) birthday present

Standardized Test Practice: Writing (Grades 3–4) © 2008 by Michael Priestley, Scholastic Teaching Resources

13. In the sentence below, which underlined word is *not* spelled correctly?

The <u>police</u> were <u>really</u> <u>surprized</u> when the <u>thief</u> turned himself in.
   Ⓐ   Ⓑ   Ⓒ   Ⓓ

14. Which sentence is written correctly?

Ⓐ   Keri is politer than her brother Taylor.

Ⓑ   Keri is politest than her brother Taylor.

Ⓒ   Keri is more politer than her brother Taylor.

Ⓓ   Keri is more polite than her brother Taylor.

15. What is the *best* way to combine the sentences below?

Danny plays on the hockey team.

Lindsey plays on the hockey team.

Ⓐ   On the hockey team, Danny and Lindsey play.

Ⓑ   Danny and Lindsey play on the hockey team.

Ⓒ   Danny plays on the hockey team, and Lindsey plays on the hockey team.

Ⓓ   Danny plays on the hockey team and Lindsey.

16. Which sentence is written correctly?

Ⓐ   Jason and I rode our bikes to school.

Ⓑ   Jason and me rode our bikes to school.

Ⓒ   I and Jason rode our bikes to school.

Ⓓ   Me and Jason rode our bikes to school.

Score: _____ /16

Name .... Date ....

> **Read the article "Paintball." Choose the word or words that correctly fit in each blank for questions 1–4.**

Paintball

Have you __(1)__ of a sport called paintball? More than 10 million people in the United States play this sport. In most games, two teams play against each other. A person who gets hit or marked by a paintball is knocked out of the game. Usually, the goal of a game is to capture a flag or to eliminate all of the other __(2)__ from the game.

Where did paintball come from? This sport was invented by three friends in __(3)__. The first game took place in 1981. The players used paintball markers that were __(4)__ used by foresters to mark trees. Since that first game, many new kinds of paintball guns have been invented.

1. **Which answer goes in blank 1?**

Ⓐ heared

Ⓑ heard

Ⓒ hear

Ⓓ hearing

2. **Which answer goes in blank 2?**

Ⓐ team's players

Ⓑ teams' players

Ⓒ teams player's

Ⓓ team's player's

3. **Which answer goes in blank 3?**

Ⓐ new hampshire

Ⓑ new Hampshire

Ⓒ New hampshire

Ⓓ New Hampshire

4. **Which answer goes in blank 4?**

Ⓐ original

Ⓑ originly

Ⓒ originally

Ⓓ most original

Standardized Test Practice: Writing (Grades 3–4) © 2008 by Michael Priestley, Scholastic Teaching Resources

Name ....   Date ....

> **Read the letter from Darnell. Choose the word or words that correctly fit in each blank for questions 5–8.**

October 22

Dear Grandma,

Last weekend we took a trip to a farm. It was really fun. Our plan was just to buy some corn. But that __(5)__ what we did. First we found out we could pick our own apples at the farm. So we filled a few bags with ripe red apples. Next we __(6)__ some pumpkins. (You know how Dad likes to carve pumpkins for Halloween!) Then we spotted the corn maze. That was the __(7)__ thing at the farm! A corn maze is made in a cornfield with many different paths. You go in one end and try to find your way through the corn to get out the other end. I was the only one in our family who found the way through. Everyone else gave up.

Then, after all that fun, we forgot to buy the corn!

__(8)__

Darnell

5. Which answer goes in blank 5?

Ⓐ was'nt

Ⓑ wasnt'

Ⓒ wasn't

Ⓓ wasnot

6. Which answer goes in blank 6?

Ⓐ buy

Ⓑ buyed

Ⓒ was buying

Ⓓ bought

7. Which answer goes in blank 7?

Ⓐ goodest

Ⓑ best

Ⓒ betterest

Ⓓ bestest

8. Which answer goes in blank 8?

Ⓐ with love

Ⓑ With Love,

Ⓒ with Love,

Ⓓ With love,

PRACTICE 28

Editing Practice B

9. Which is a complete sentence?

Ⓐ On the way to the beach.

Ⓑ Our car had a flat tire.

Ⓒ A spare tire in the trunk.

Ⓓ Fixing the tire by the road.

10. Read the following sentence:

Charles wants to climb Mount Mansfield, or he may hike to Sterling Pond instead.

What is the correct way to rewrite the sentence?

Ⓐ Charles wants to climb Mount Mansfield, and he may hike to Sterling Pond instead.

Ⓑ Charles wants to climb Mount Mansfield, so he may hike to Sterling Pond instead.

Ⓒ Charles wants to climb Mount Mansfield, because he may hike to Sterling Pond instead.

Ⓓ Leave as is.

11. In the sentence below, which word is the simple predicate?

At exactly eight o'clock, Hannah's alarm clock buzzed.

Ⓐ exactly   Ⓒ clock

Ⓑ Hannah's   Ⓓ buzzed

12. Which sentence below is written correctly?

Ⓐ How old is this house? asked Nell.

Ⓑ "How old is this house? asked Nell."

Ⓒ "How old is this house?" asked Nell.

Ⓓ "How old is this house" asked Nell?

Standardized Test Practice: Writing (Grades 3–4) © 2008 by Michael Priestley, Scholastic Teaching Resources